CONTENTS

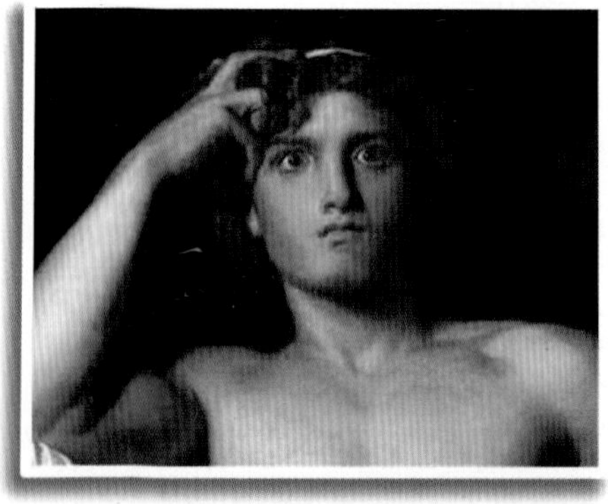

Graced with golden locks and a fine, strong body, Achilles was said to be the most handsome Greek hero of them all.

In Greek mythology, Achilles was born a half god to the sea nymph Thetis and the mortal man Peleus. Legend had it that Thetis tried to make Achilles a whole god by dipping him in the River Styx as an infant. The only place not touched by the sacred waters was where she held him by the heel—his weak spot.

PROPHECIES

As a famed youth, Achilles was the subject of many prophecies, the first of which said his life would take one of two paths—an early death on a foreign field of battle, or an undistinguished old age in Achaea (Greece).

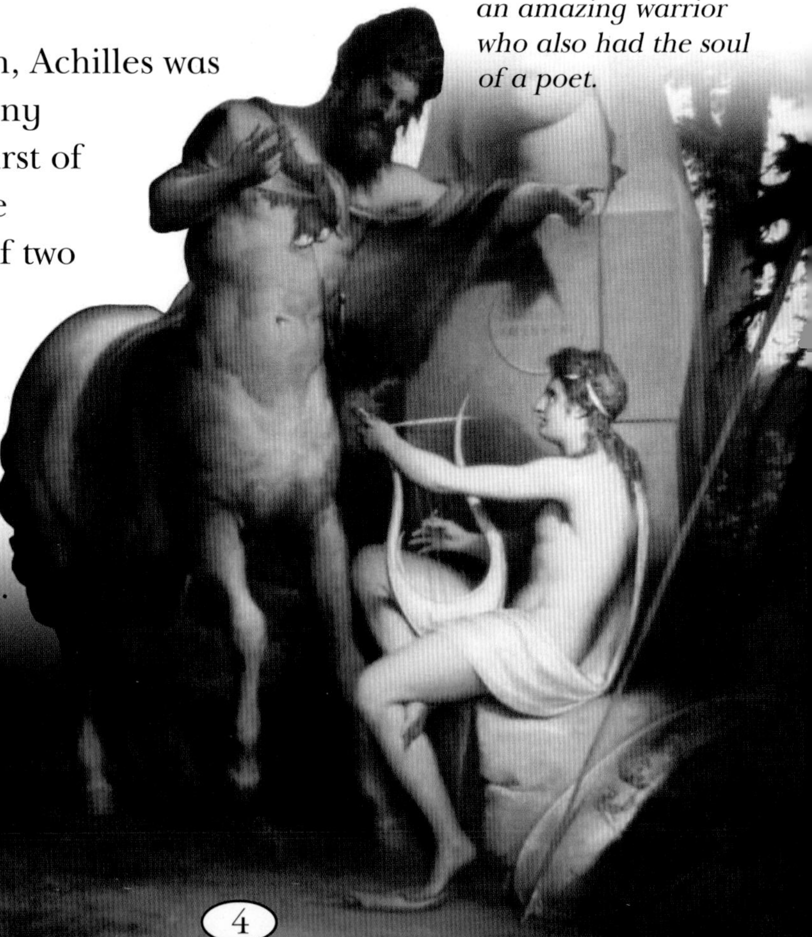

Schooled by the centaur Chiron, Achilles grew up to be an amazing warrior who also had the soul of a poet.

GRAPHIC MYTHICAL HEROES

ACHILLES
AND THE TROJAN WAR

BY GARY JEFFREY
ILLUSTRATED BY NICK SPENDER

Gareth Stevens
Publishing

Please visit our website, www.garethstevens.com.
For a free color catalog of all our high-quality books,
call toll free 1-800-542-2595 or fax 1-877-542-2596.

Library of Congress Cataloging-in-Publication Data

Jeffrey, Gary.
Achilles and the Trojan War / Gary Jeffrey.
p. cm. — (Graphic mythical heroes)
Includes index.
ISBN 978-1-4339-7508-0 (pbk.)
ISBN 978-1-4339-7509-7 (6-pack)
ISBN 978-1-4339-7507-3 (library binding)
1. Achilles (Greek mythology)—Juvenile literature. 2. Trojan War—
Juvenile literature. I. Title.
BL820.A22J44 2012
398.20938'01—dc23
                                    2011045596

First Edition

Published in 2013 by
Gareth Stevens Publishing
111 East 14th Street, Suite 349
New York, NY 10003

Copyright © 2013 David West Books

Designed by David West Books

Printed in China

CPSIA compliance information: Batch #DWS12GS: For further information contact Gareth Stevens, New York, New York at 1-800-542-2595.

The prize of Helen's love was offered to Paris as a bribe by the goddess Aphrodite. Zeus had asked Paris to judge who should win a golden apple in a contest between her and two other goddesses.

WAR WITH TROY

When the Trojan prince Paris spirited away Helen, the wife of Spartan king Menelaus, war was declared on Troy. A thousand ships were sent there. A seer foretold that Troy would not be taken unless Achilles fought alongside the other Greek heroes. Achilles commanded 50 ships and more than 2,000 warriors called Myrmidons.

A FEUD

It took eight years after landing to finally surround the great walled city of Troy. As they prepared to lay siege, a quarrel broke out between the Greek general Agamemnon and Achilles over a war trophy. Achilles refused to fight and took his men out of the battle. Emboldened, the Trojan king, Priam, ordered Paris's brother Hector to go out with an army to drive the Greeks back to their ships. Alarmed, Achilles's lieutenant, Patroclus, begged his friend and commander to let him lead the Myrmidons into battle and save the day…

Agamemnon took the Trojan slave Briseis away from Achilles to have as his own. This hurt the warrior's pride and roused his famous anger.

5

ACHILLES BATTLES HECTOR

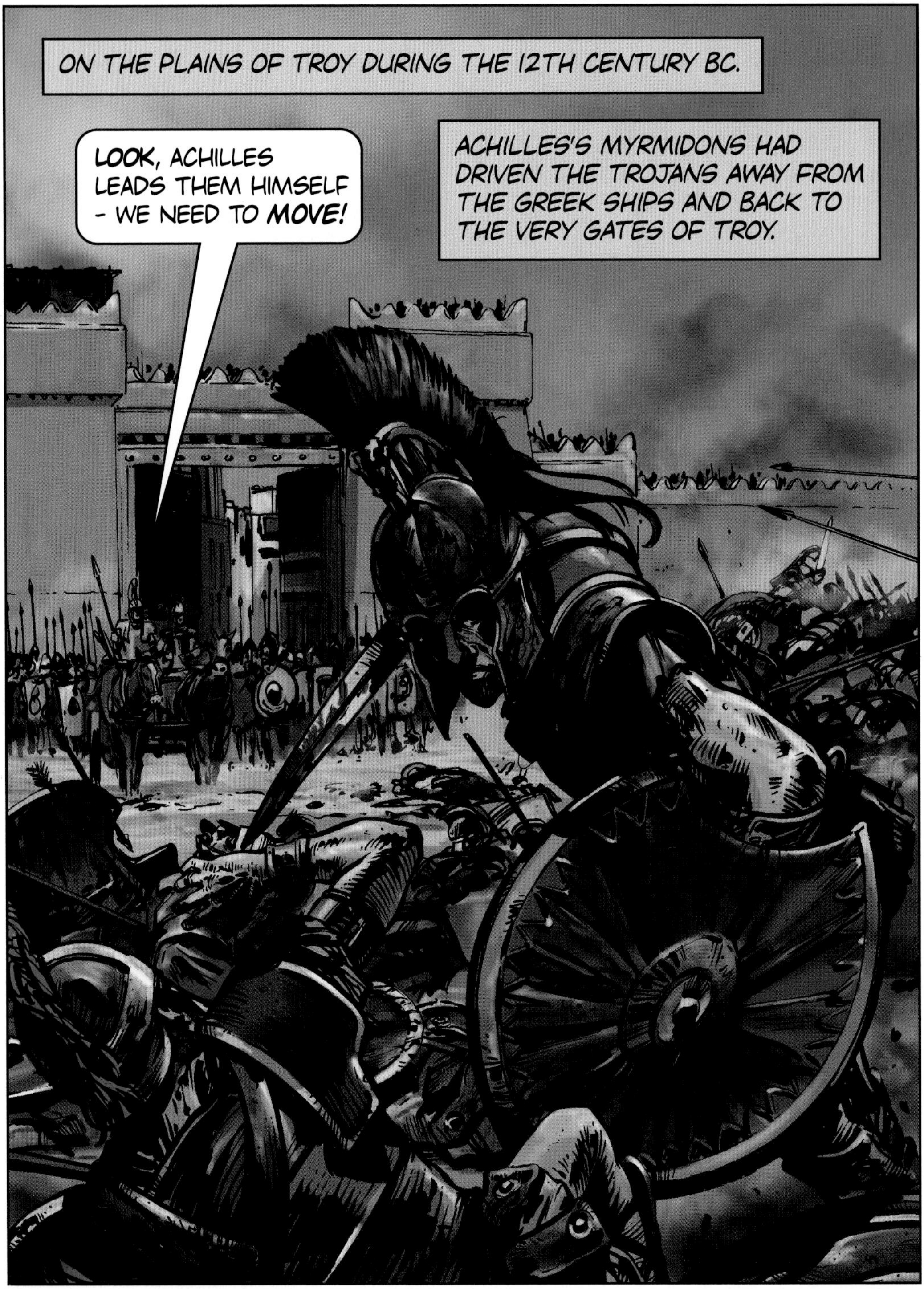
ON THE PLAINS OF TROY DURING THE 12TH CENTURY BC.
LOOK, ACHILLES LEADS THEM HIMSELF - WE NEED TO MOVE!
ACHILLES'S MYRMIDONS HAD DRIVEN THE TROJANS AWAY FROM THE GREEK SHIPS AND BACK TO THE VERY GATES OF TROY.

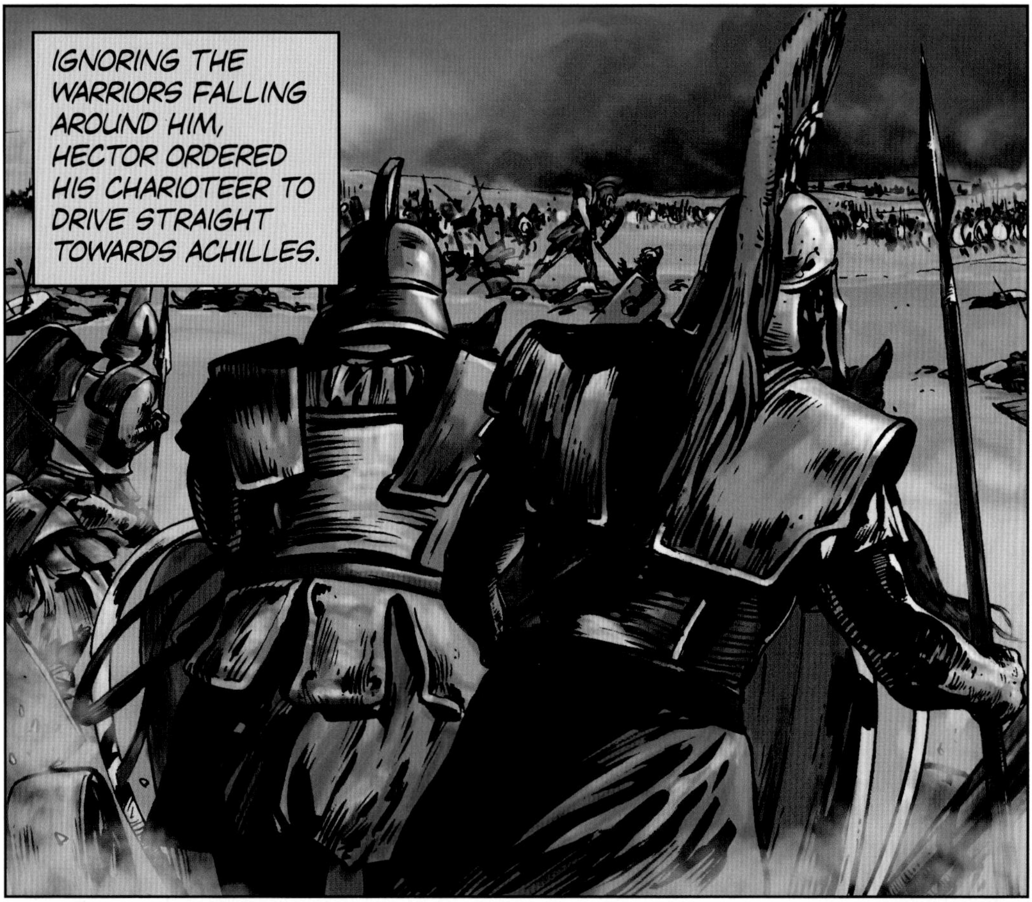
IGNORING THE WARRIORS FALLING AROUND HIM, HECTOR ORDERED HIS CHARIOTEER TO DRIVE STRAIGHT TOWARDS ACHILLES.

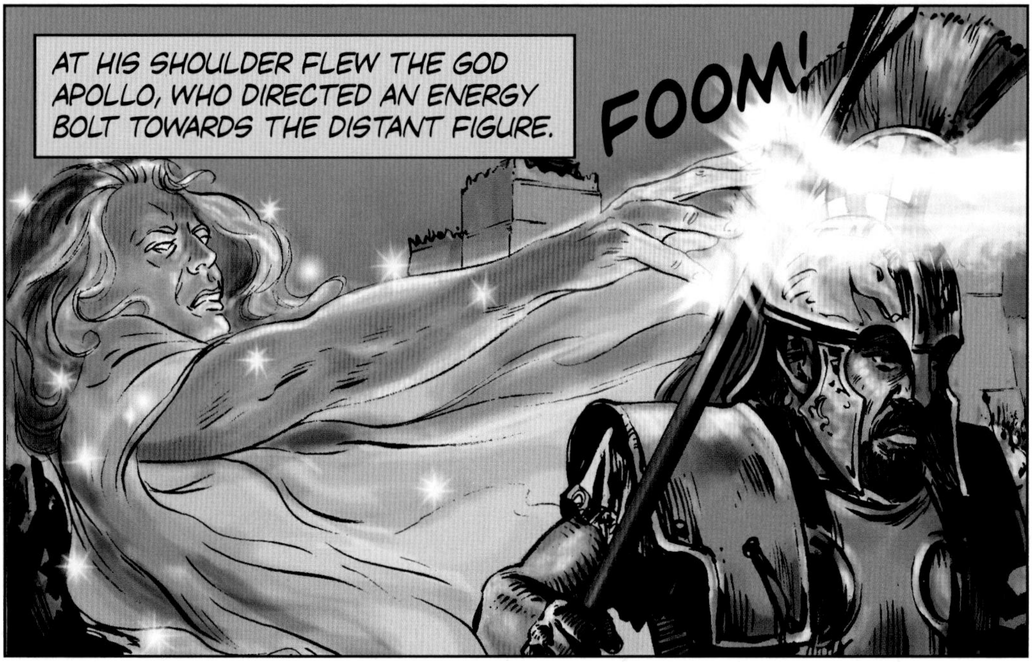
AT HIS SHOULDER FLEW THE GOD APOLLO, WHO DIRECTED AN ENERGY BOLT TOWARDS THE DISTANT FIGURE.
FOOM!

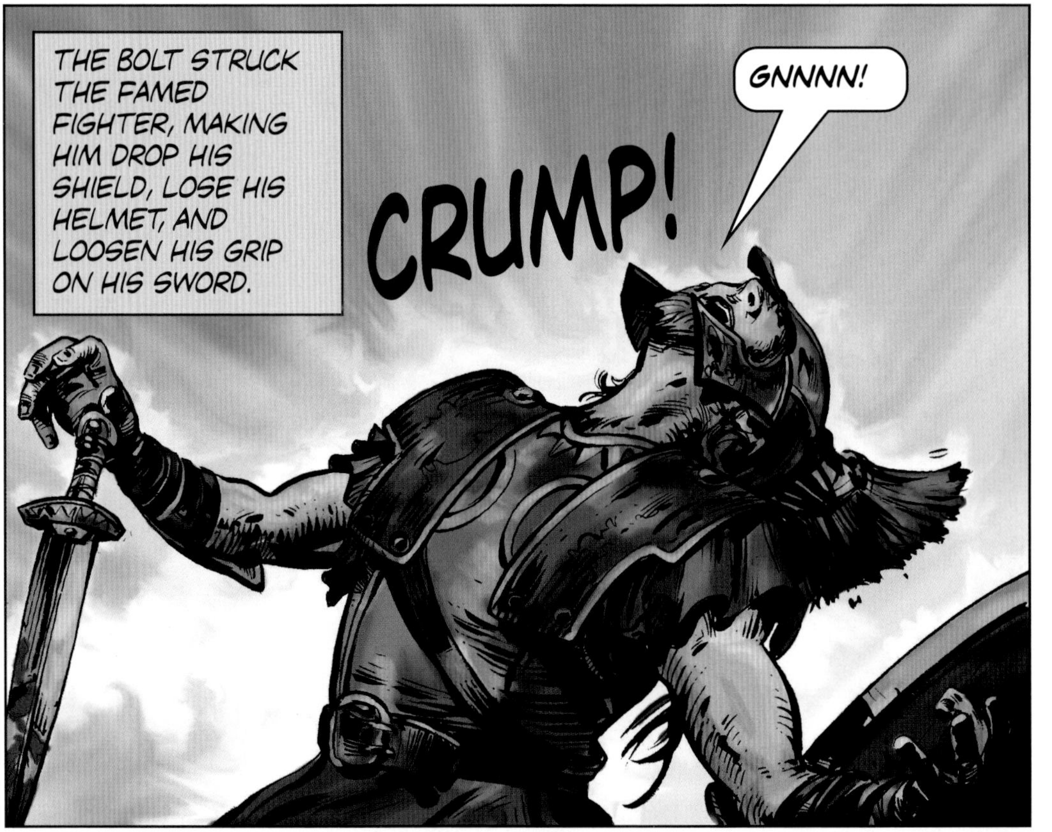
THE BOLT STRUCK THE FAMED FIGHTER, MAKING HIM DROP HIS SHIELD, LOSE HIS HELMET, AND LOOSEN HIS GRIP ON HIS SWORD.
CRUMP!
GNNNN!

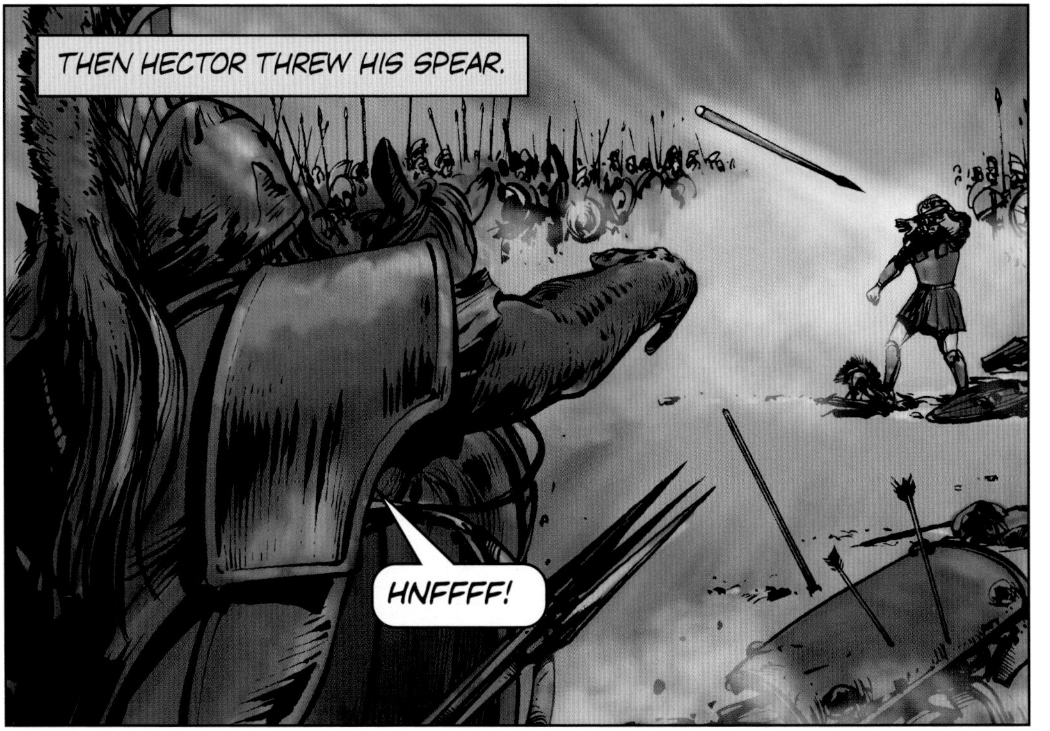
THEN HECTOR THREW HIS SPEAR.
HNFFFF!

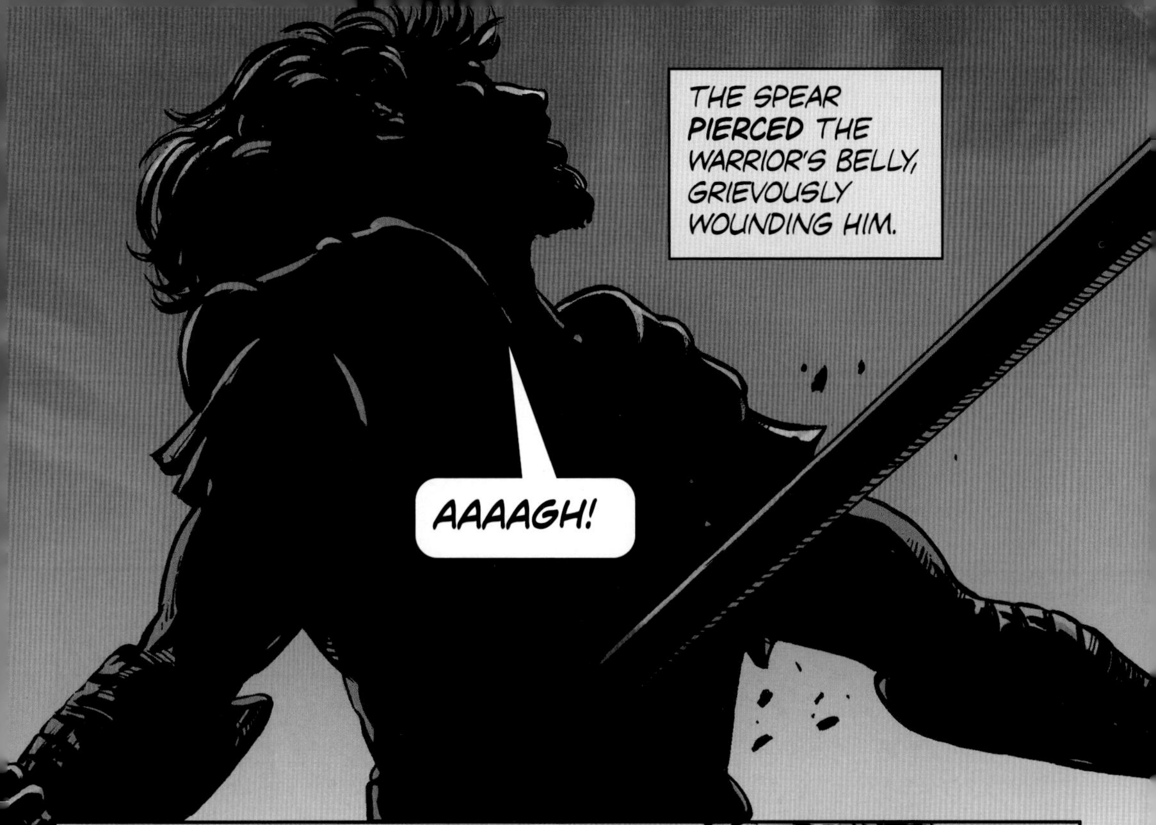
THE SPEAR **PIERCED** THE WARRIOR'S BELLY, GRIEVOUSLY WOUNDING HIM.
AAAAGH!

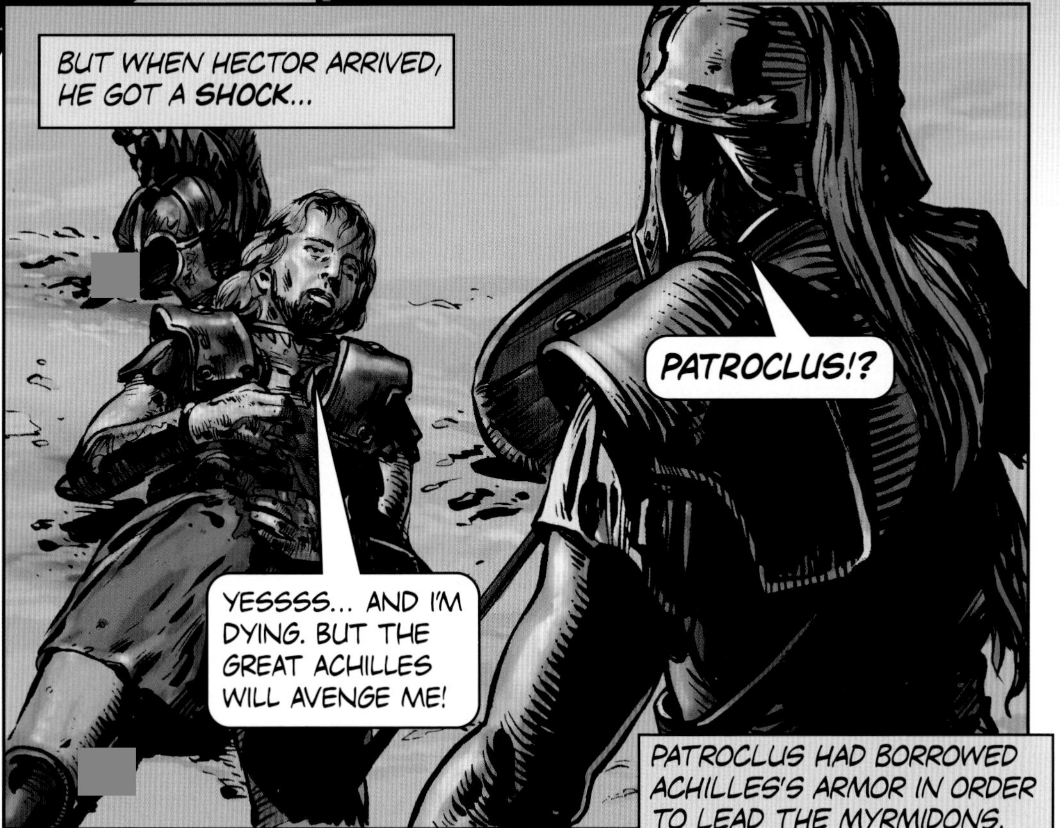
BUT WHEN HECTOR ARRIVED, HE GOT A **SHOCK**...
PATROCLUS!?
YESSSS... AND I'M DYING. BUT THE GREAT ACHILLES WILL AVENGE ME!
PATROCLUS HAD BORROWED ACHILLES'S ARMOR IN ORDER TO LEAD THE MYRMIDONS.

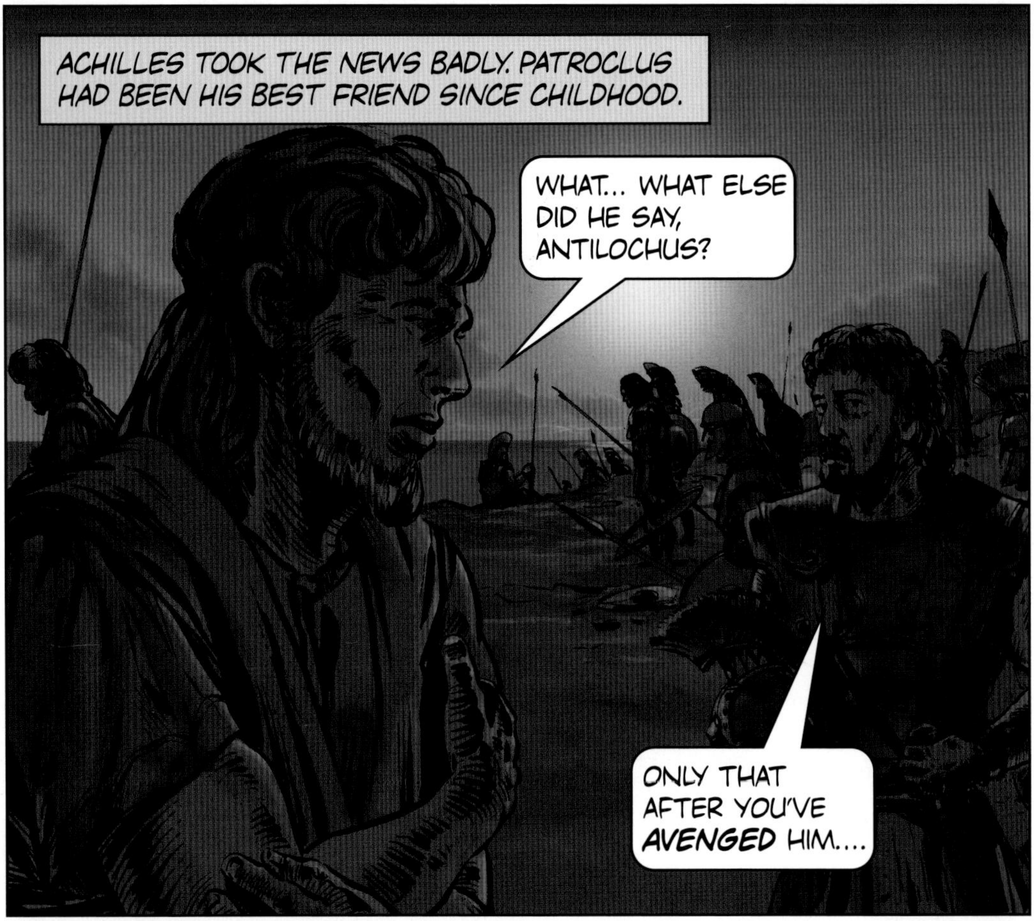
ACHILLES TOOK THE NEWS BADLY. PATROCLUS HAD BEEN HIS BEST FRIEND SINCE CHILDHOOD.
WHAT... WHAT ELSE DID HE SAY, ANTILOCHUS?
ONLY THAT AFTER YOU'VE AVENGED HIM....

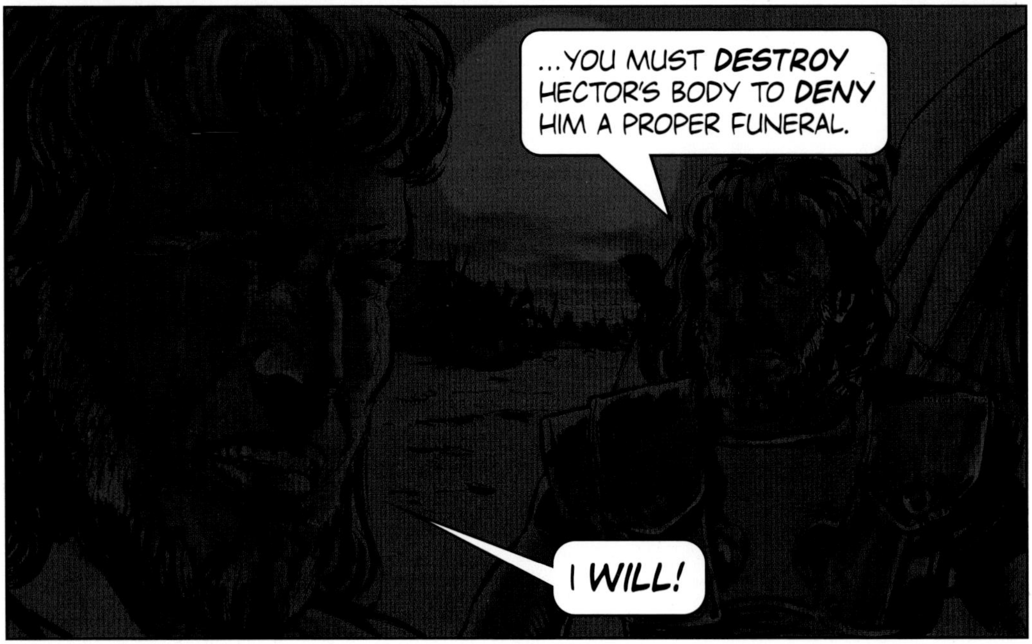
...YOU MUST DESTROY HECTOR'S BODY TO DENY HIM A PROPER FUNERAL.
I WILL!

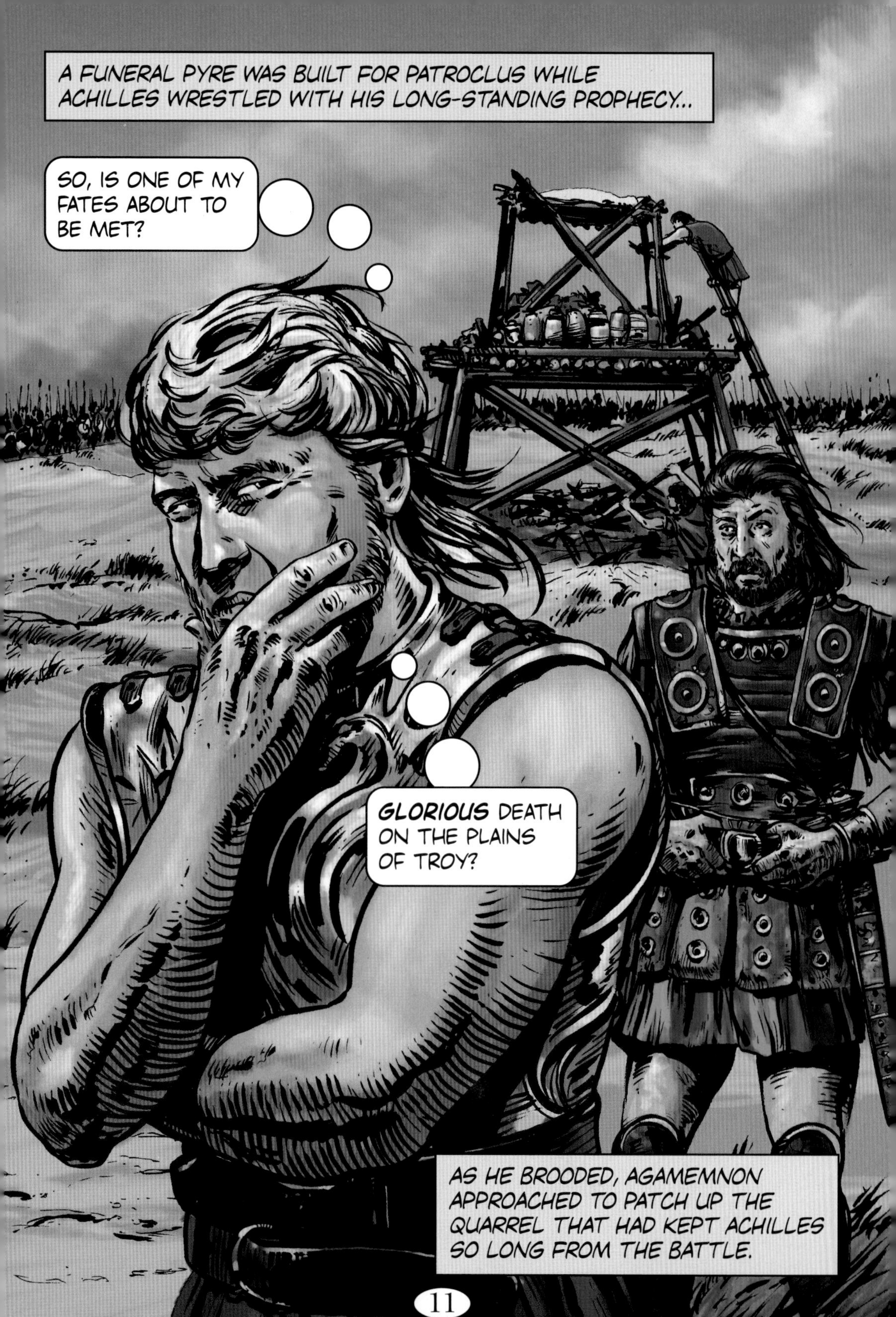
A FUNERAL PYRE WAS BUILT FOR PATROCLUS WHILE ACHILLES WRESTLED WITH HIS LONG-STANDING PROPHECY...
SO, IS ONE OF MY FATES ABOUT TO BE MET?
GLORIOUS DEATH ON THE PLAINS OF TROY?
AS HE BROODED, AGAMEMNON APPROACHED TO PATCH UP THE QUARREL THAT HAD KEPT ACHILLES SO LONG FROM THE BATTLE.

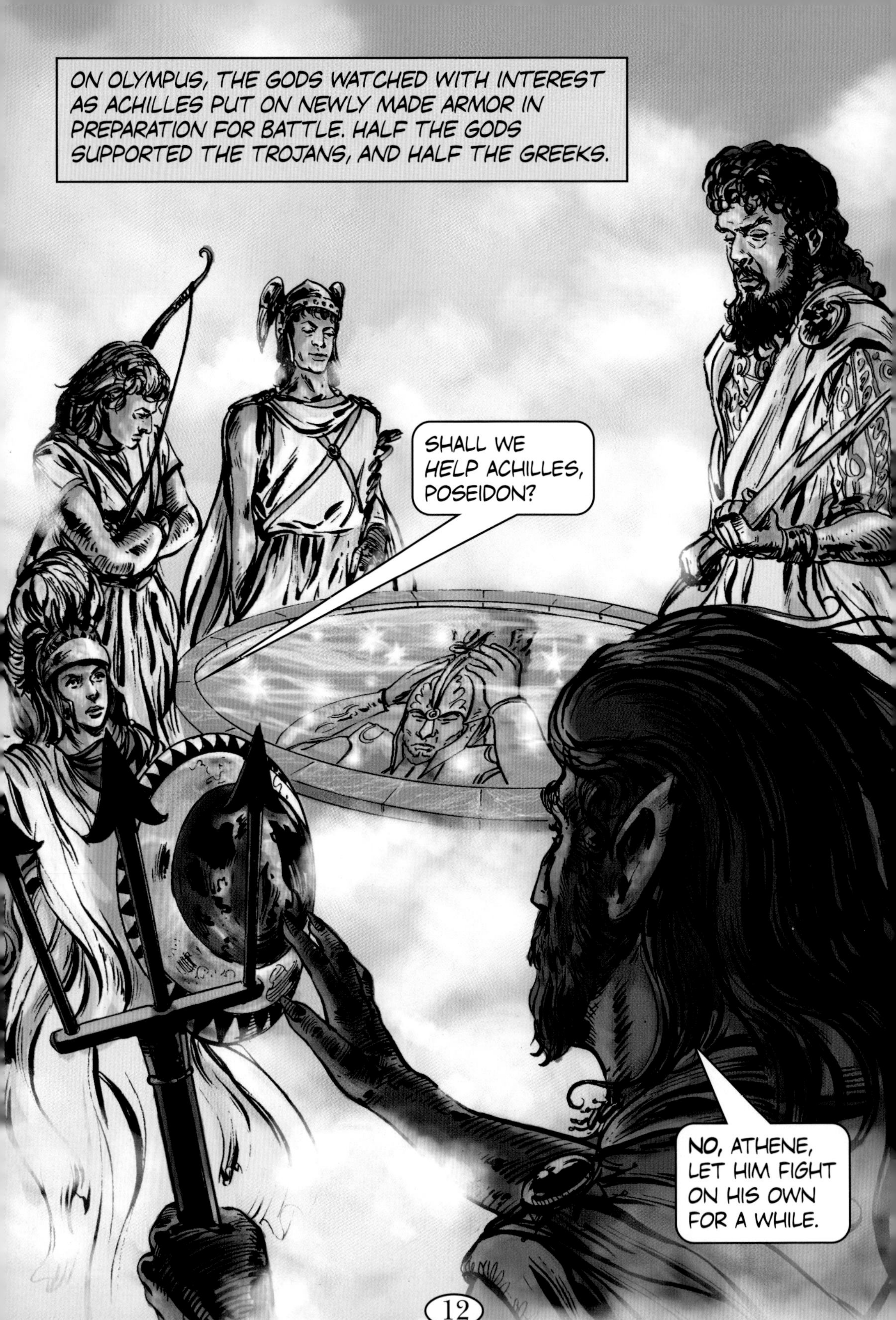
ON OLYMPUS, THE GODS WATCHED WITH INTEREST AS ACHILLES PUT ON NEWLY MADE ARMOR IN PREPARATION FOR BATTLE. HALF THE GODS SUPPORTED THE TROJANS, AND HALF THE GREEKS.
SHALL WE HELP ACHILLES, POSEIDON?
NO, ATHENE, LET HIM FIGHT ON HIS OWN FOR A WHILE.

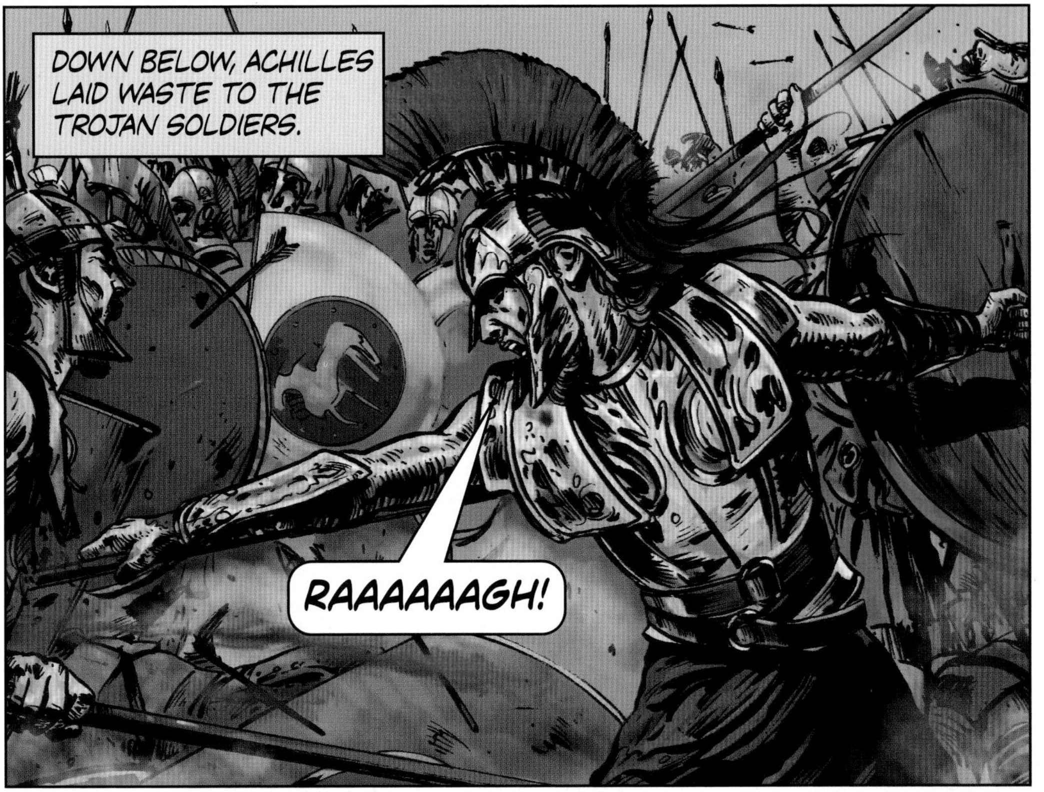
DOWN BELOW, ACHILLES LAID WASTE TO THE TROJAN SOLDIERS.
RAAAAAAGH!

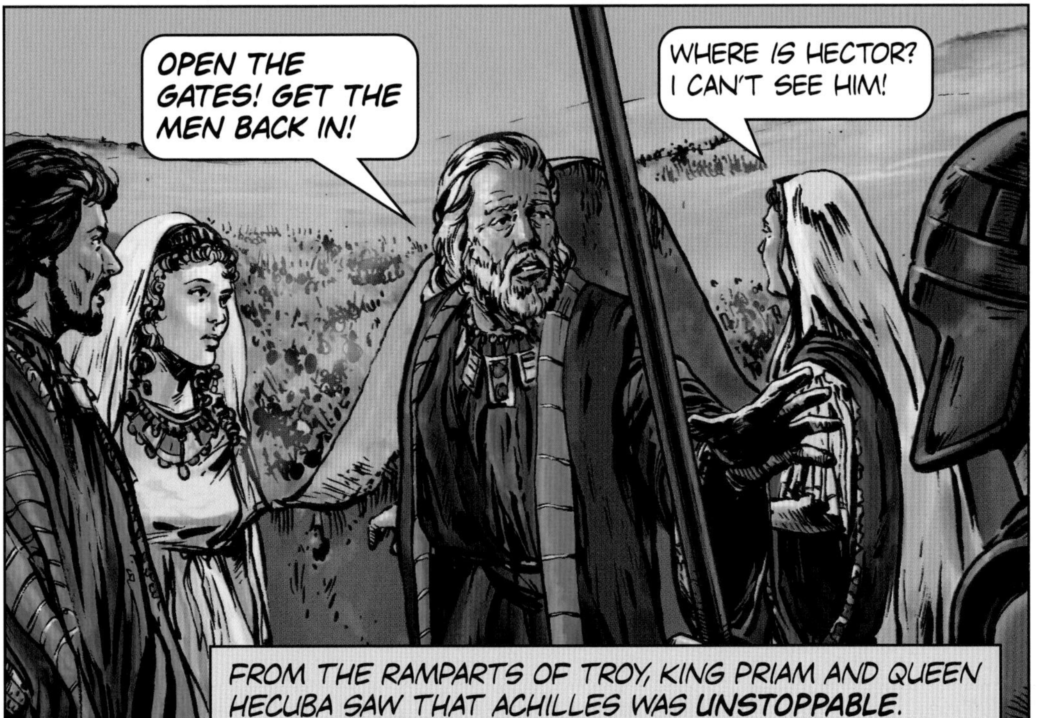
OPEN THE GATES! GET THE MEN BACK IN!
WHERE IS HECTOR? I CAN'T SEE HIM!
FROM THE RAMPARTS OF TROY, KING PRIAM AND QUEEN HECUBA SAW THAT ACHILLES WAS **UNSTOPPABLE**.

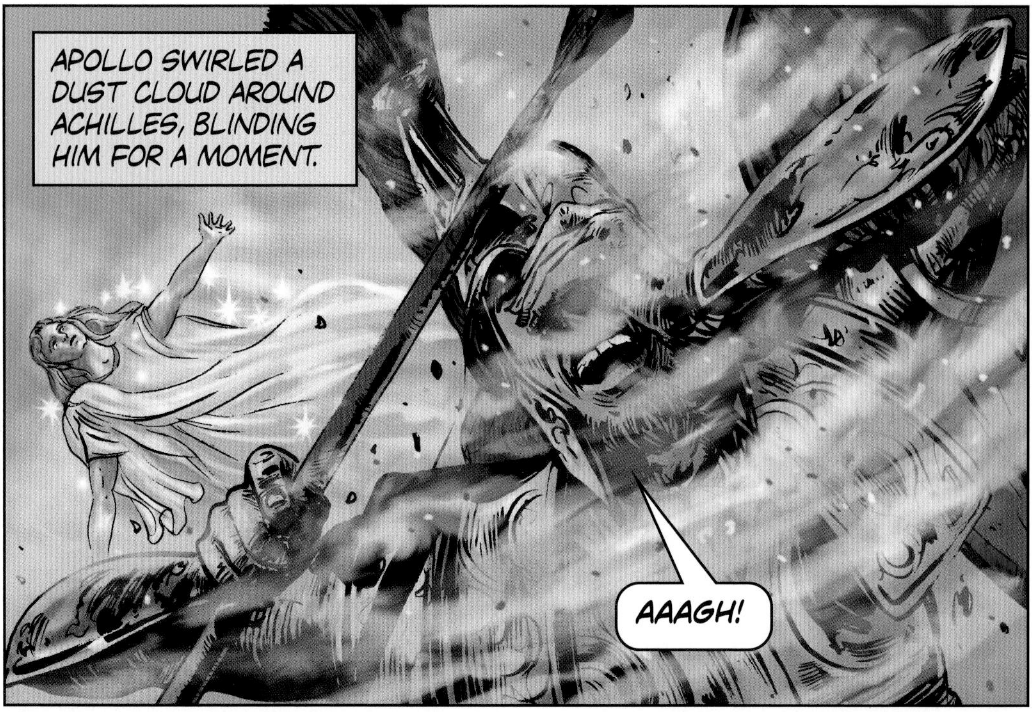
APOLLO SWIRLED A DUST CLOUD AROUND ACHILLES, BLINDING HIM FOR A MOMENT.
AAAGH!

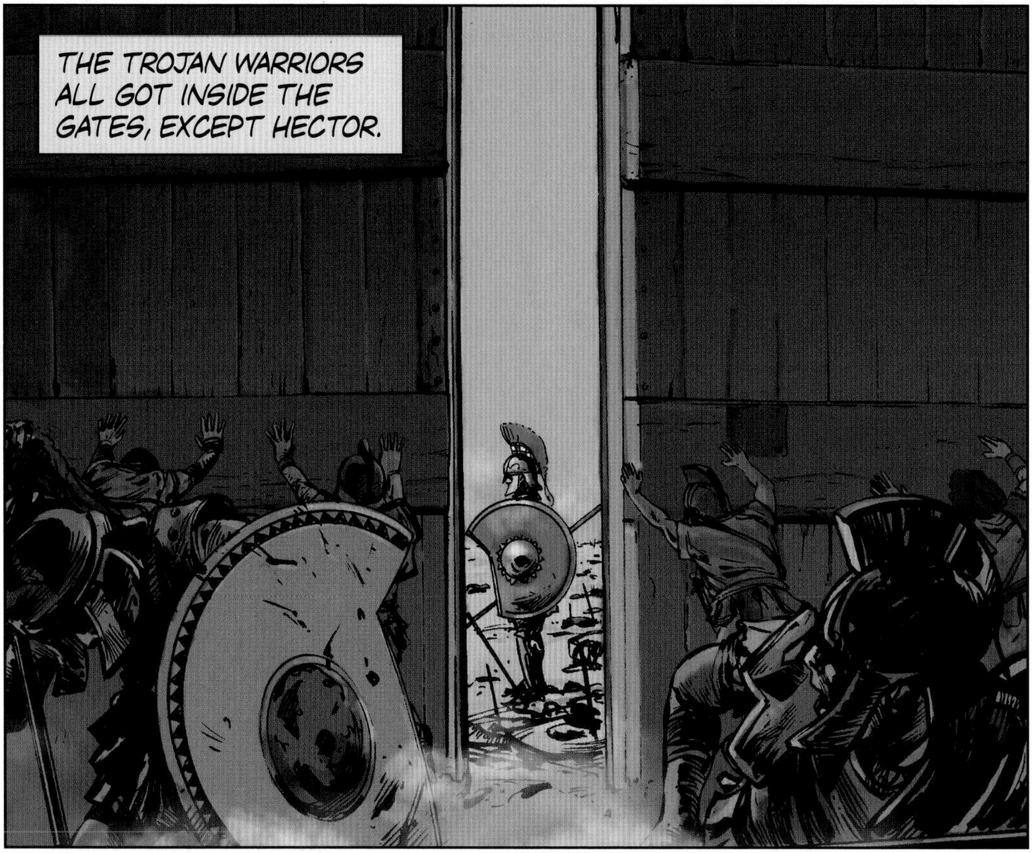
THE TROJAN WARRIORS ALL GOT INSIDE THE GATES, EXCEPT HECTOR.

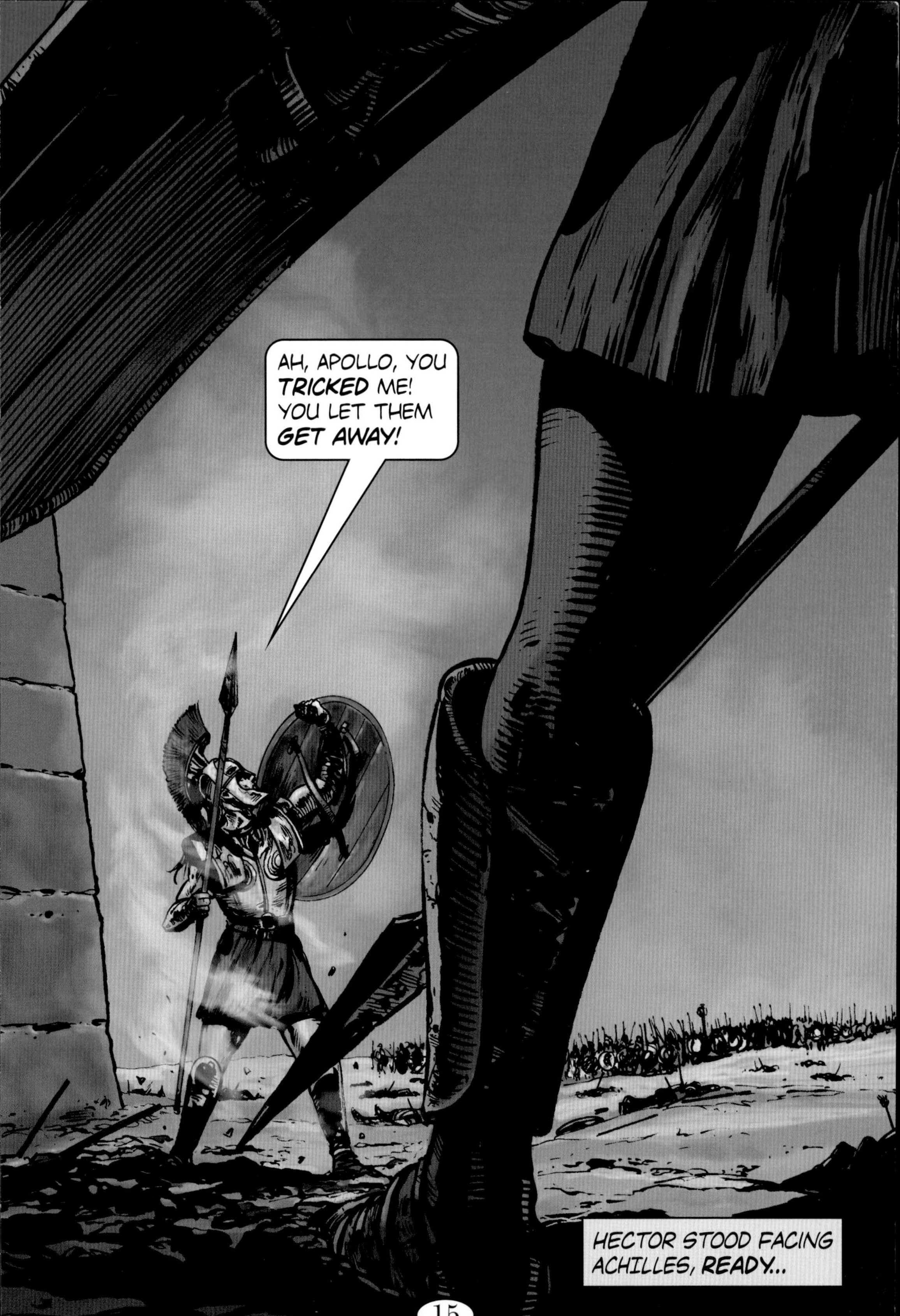
AH, APOLLO, YOU TRICKED ME! YOU LET THEM GET AWAY!
HECTOR STOOD FACING ACHILLES, READY...

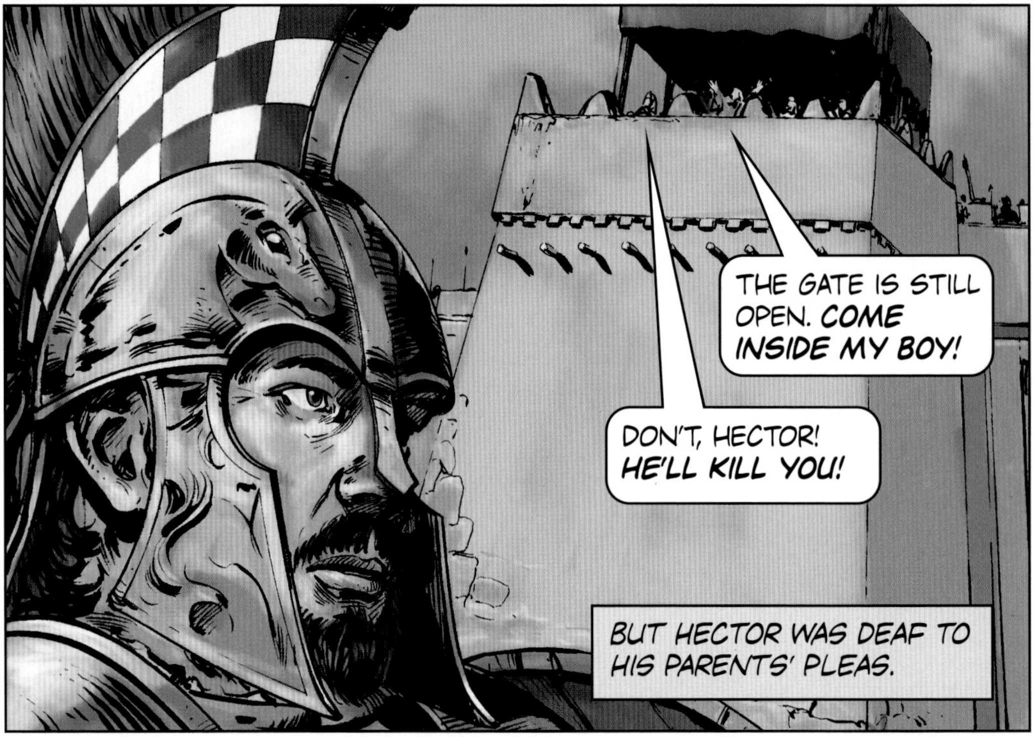
THE GATE IS STILL OPEN. COME INSIDE MY BOY!
DON'T, HECTOR! HE'LL KILL YOU!
BUT HECTOR WAS DEAF TO HIS PARENTS' PLEAS.

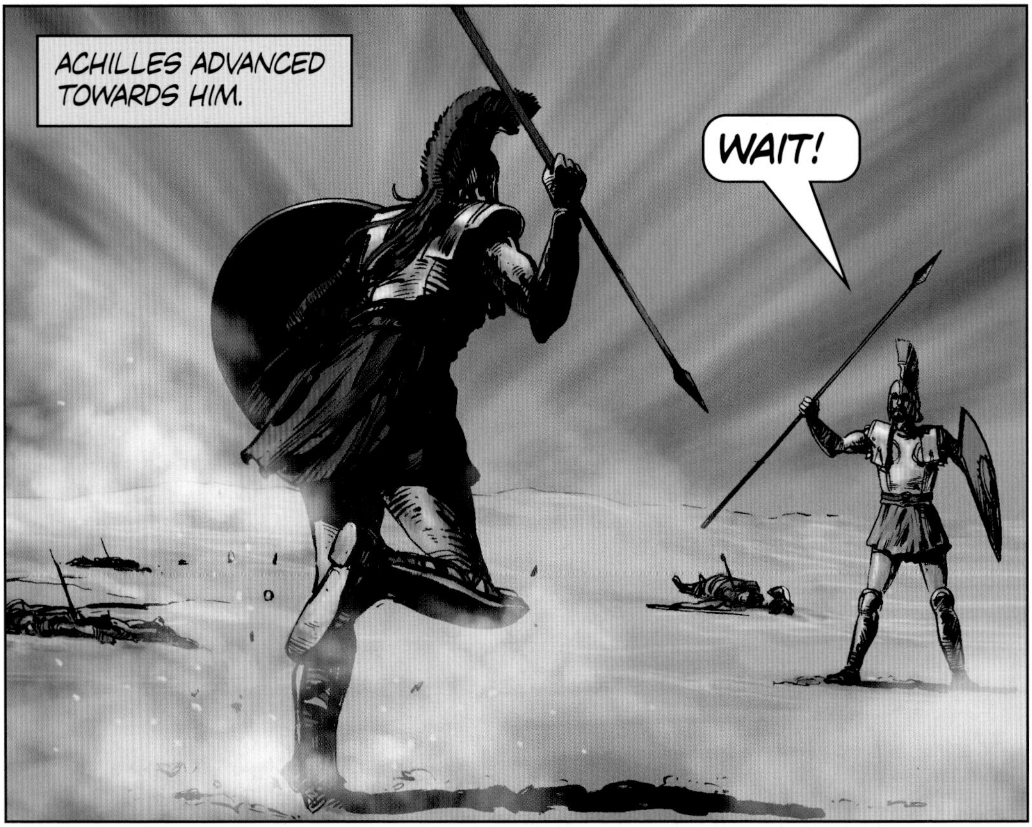
ACHILLES ADVANCED TOWARDS HIM.
WAIT!

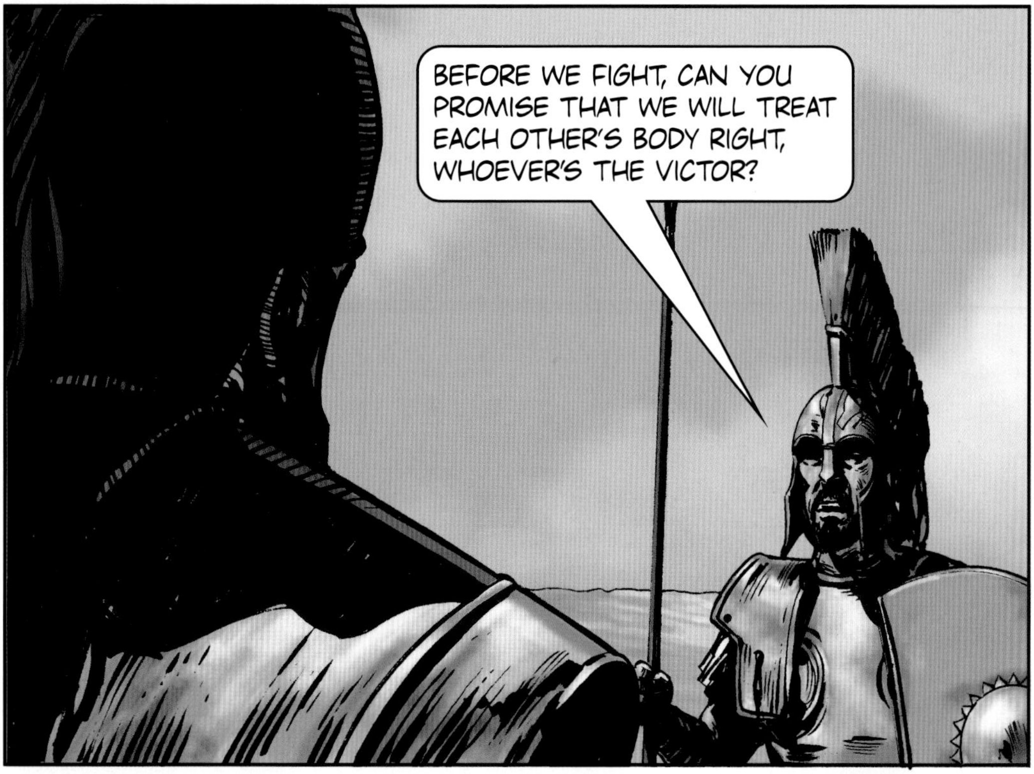
BEFORE WE FIGHT, CAN YOU PROMISE THAT WE WILL TREAT EACH OTHER'S BODY RIGHT, WHOEVER'S THE VICTOR?

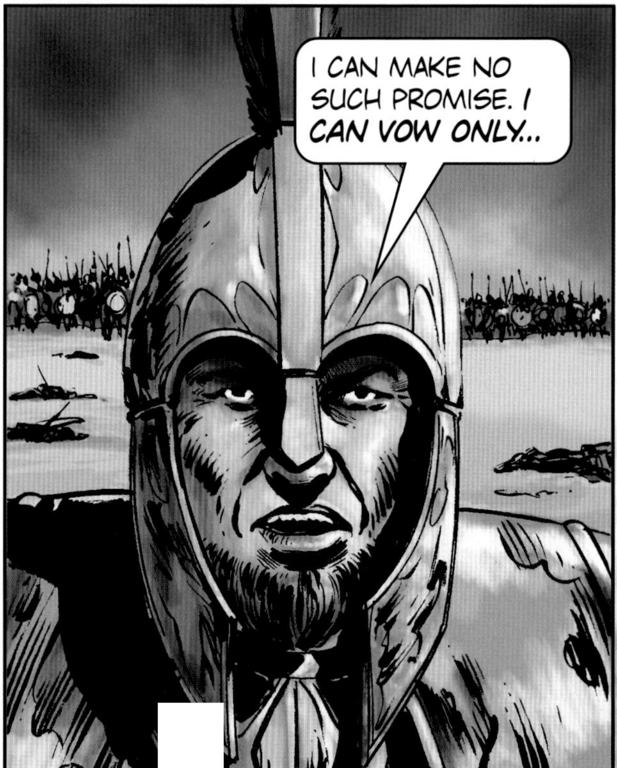
I CAN MAKE NO SUCH PROMISE. I *CAN VOW ONLY...*

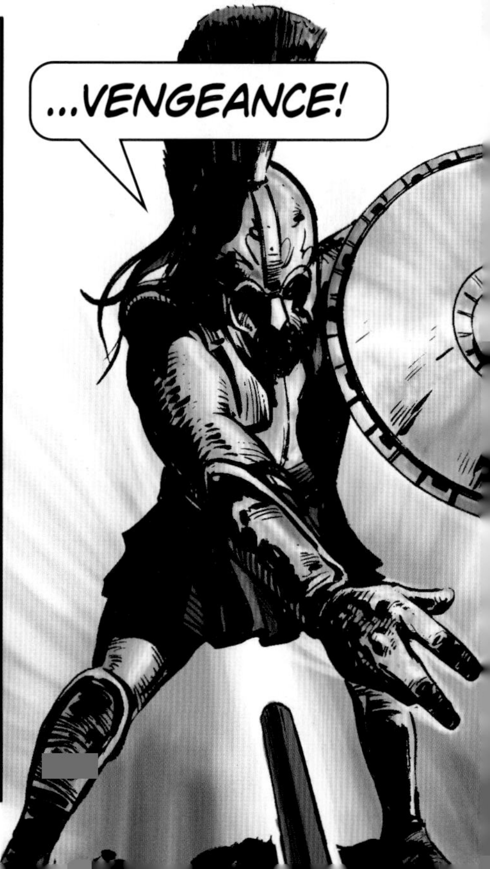
...VENGEANCE!

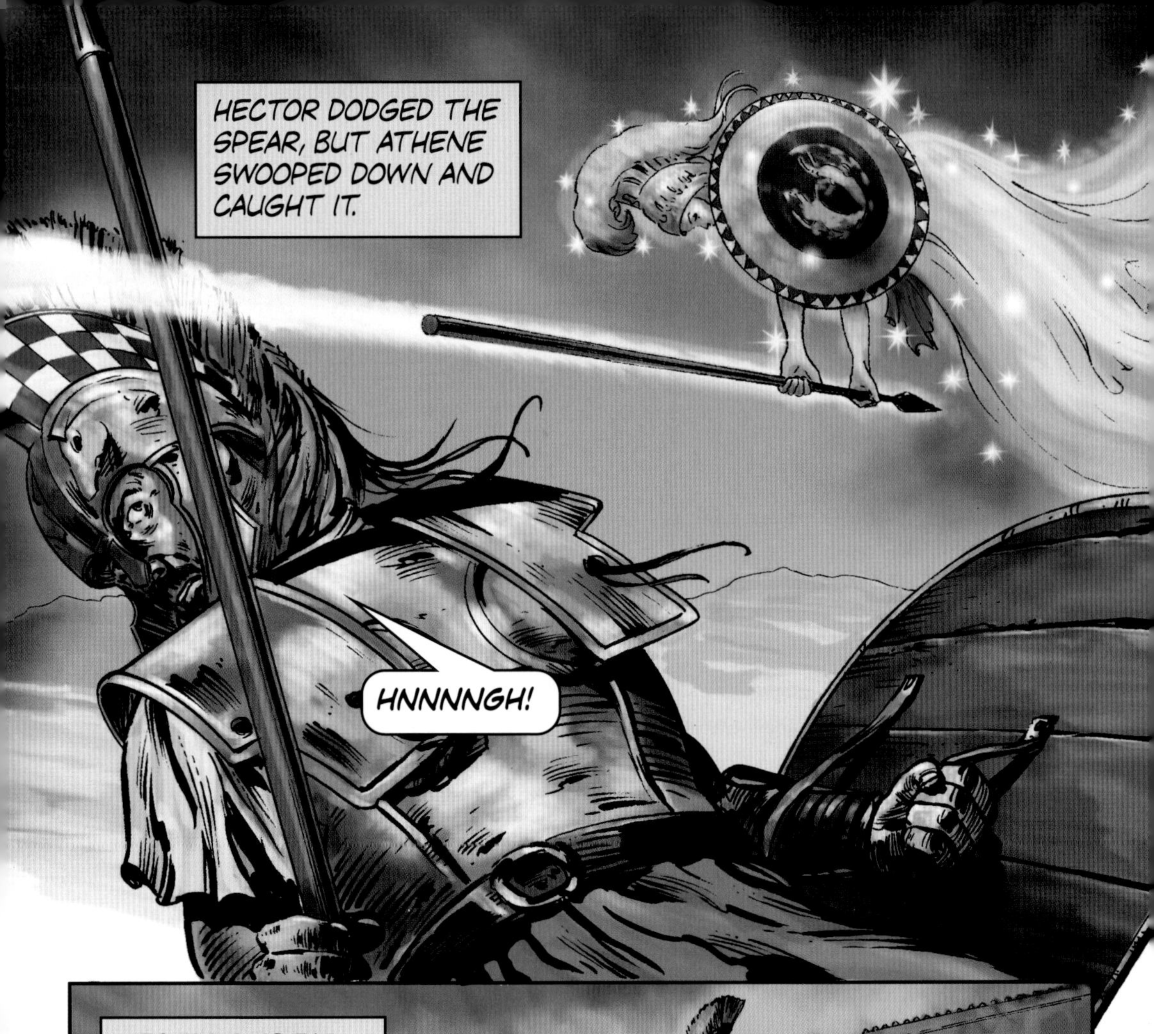
HECTOR DODGED THE SPEAR, BUT ATHENE SWOOPED DOWN AND CAUGHT IT.
HNNNNGH!

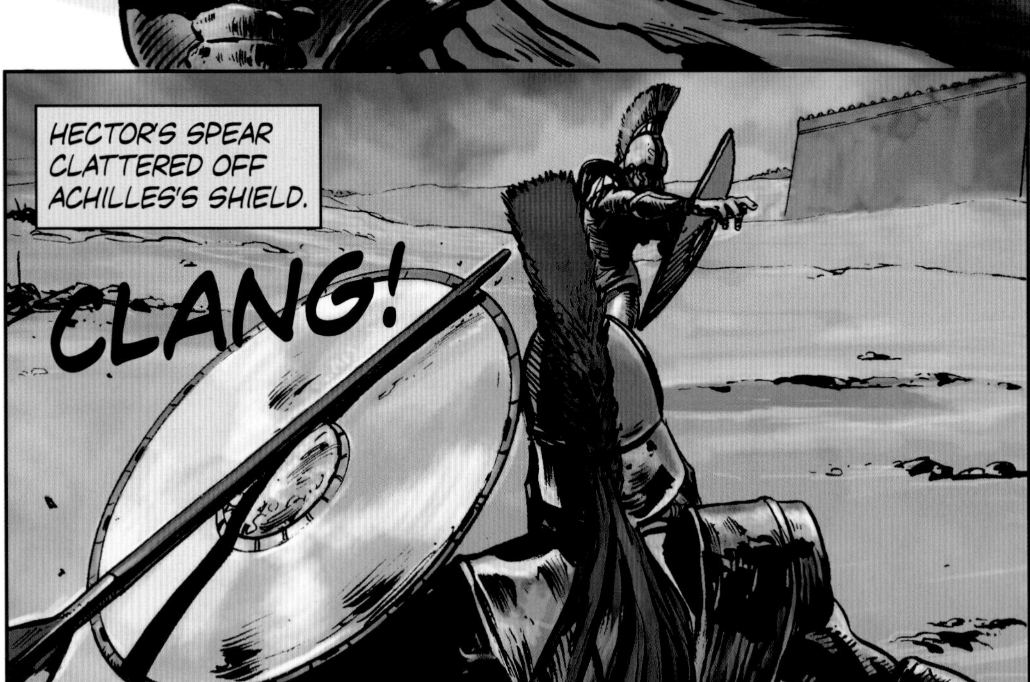
HECTOR'S SPEAR CLATTERED OFF ACHILLES'S SHIELD.
CLANG!

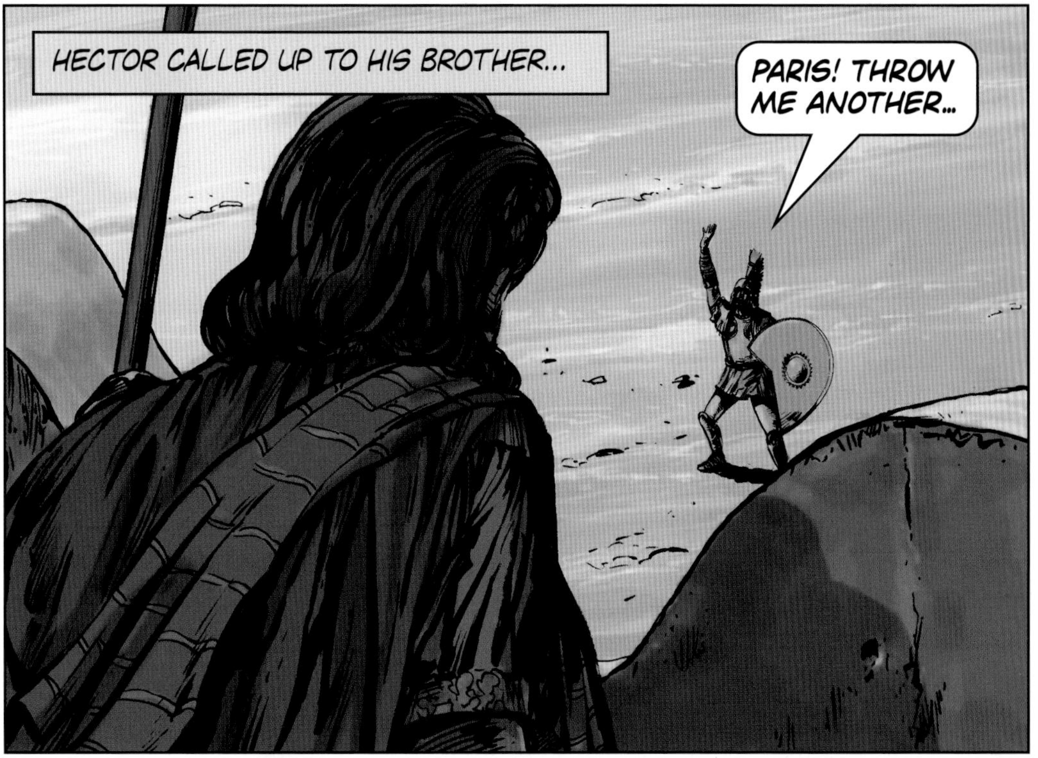
HECTOR CALLED UP TO HIS BROTHER...
PARIS! THROW ME ANOTHER...

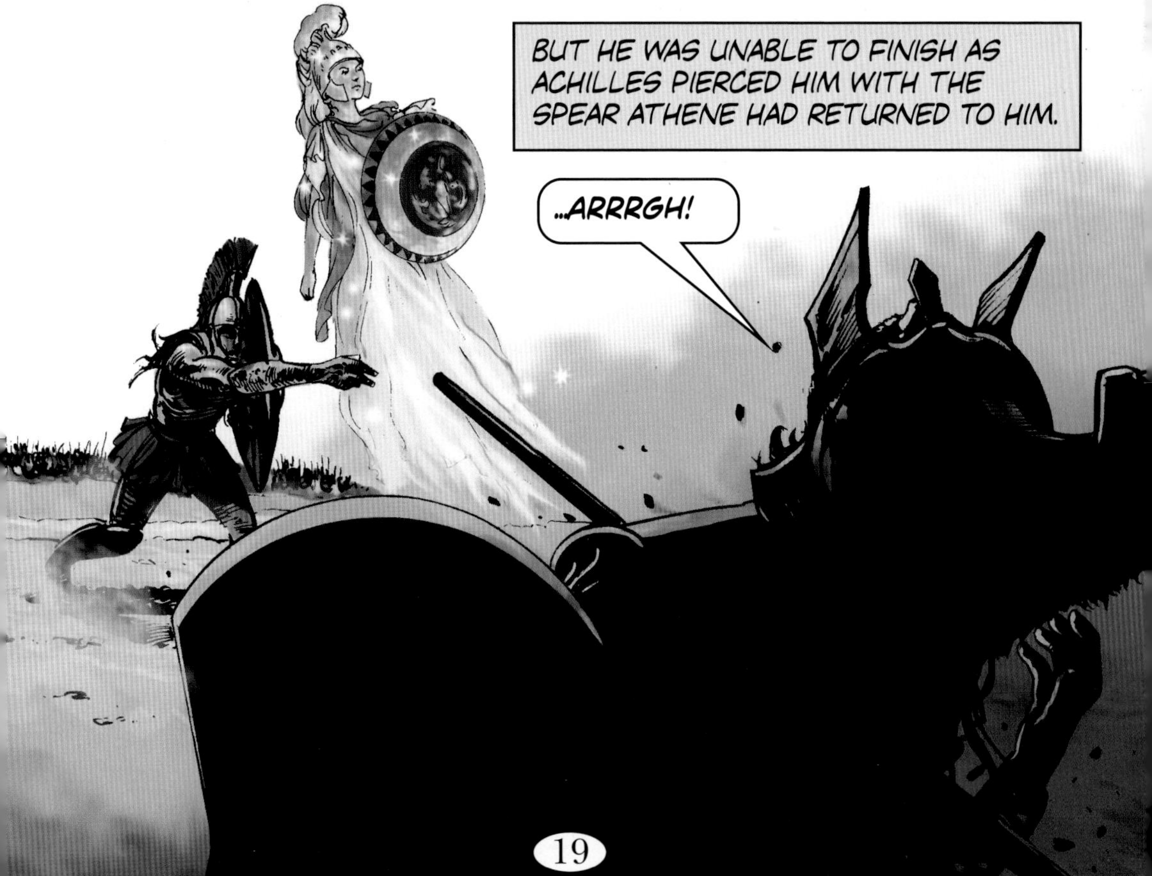
BUT HE WAS UNABLE TO FINISH AS ACHILLES PIERCED HIM WITH THE SPEAR ATHENE HAD RETURNED TO HIM.
...ARRRGH!

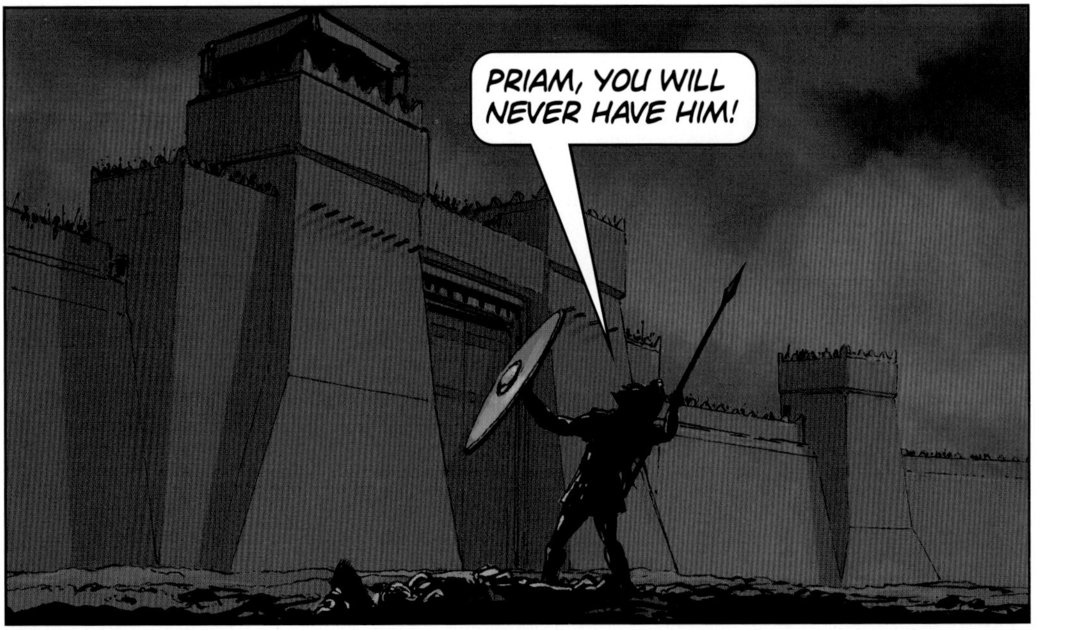
PRIAM, YOU WILL NEVER HAVE HIM!

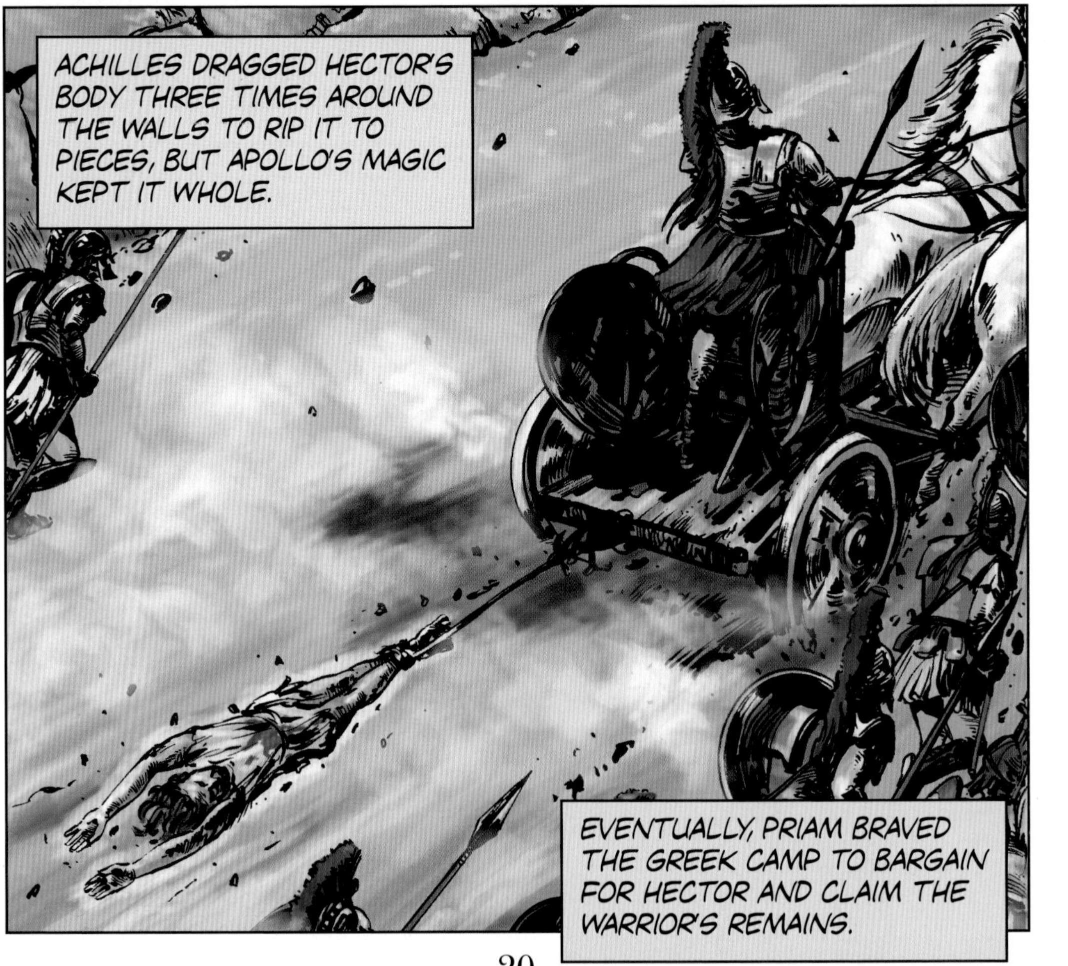
ACHILLES DRAGGED HECTOR'S BODY THREE TIMES AROUND THE WALLS TO RIP IT TO PIECES, BUT APOLLO'S MAGIC KEPT IT WHOLE.
EVENTUALLY, PRIAM BRAVED THE GREEK CAMP TO BARGAIN FOR HECTOR AND CLAIM THE WARRIOR'S REMAINS.

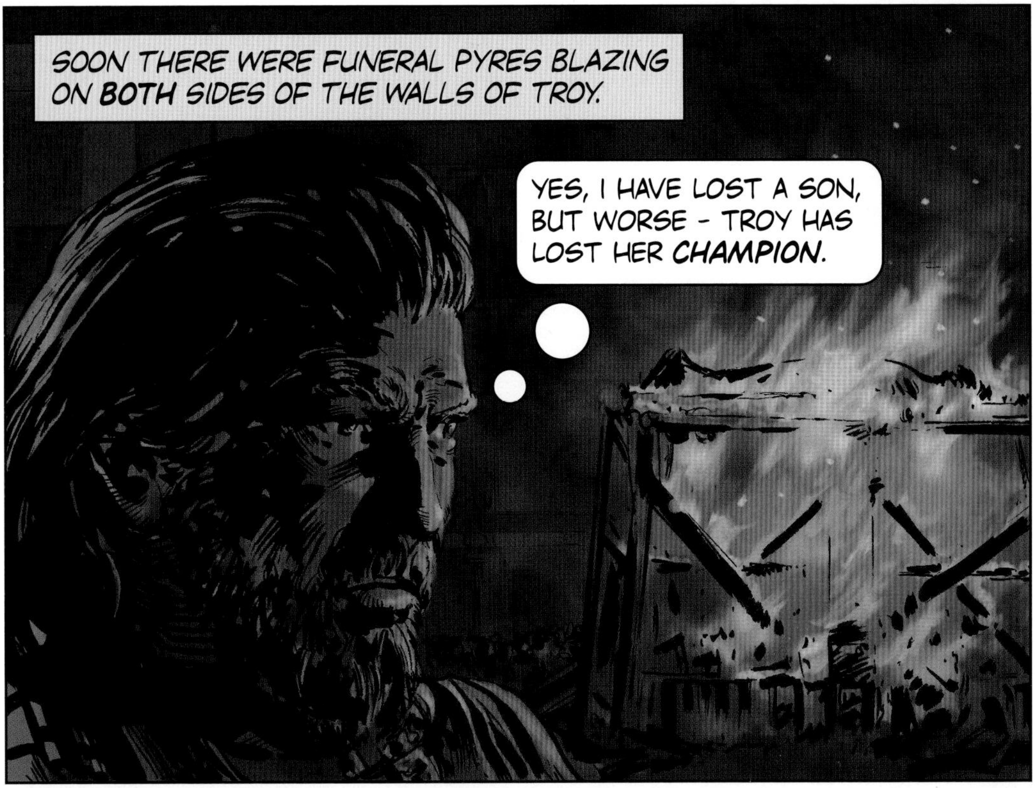
SOON THERE WERE FUNERAL PYRES BLAZING ON BOTH SIDES OF THE WALLS OF TROY.
YES, I HAVE LOST A SON, BUT WORSE - TROY HAS LOST HER CHAMPION.

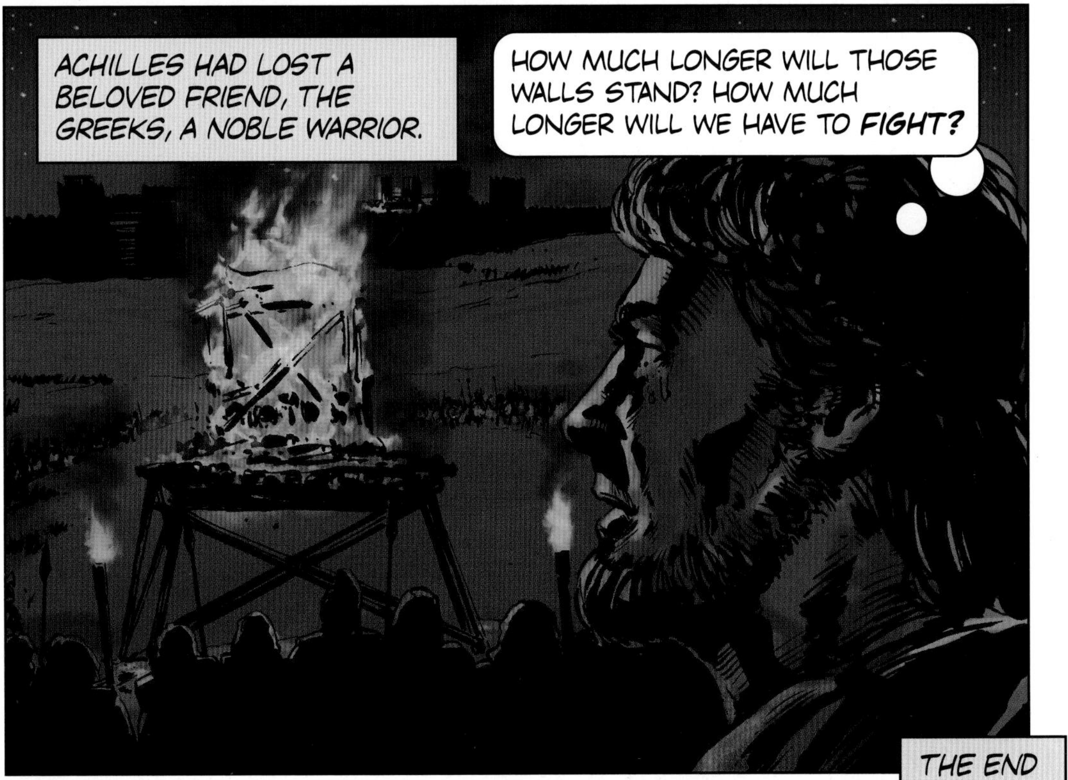
ACHILLES HAD LOST A BELOVED FRIEND, THE GREEKS, A NOBLE WARRIOR.
HOW MUCH LONGER WILL THOSE WALLS STAND? HOW MUCH LONGER WILL WE HAVE TO FIGHT?
THE END

THE DEATH OF ACHILLES

After the funeral of Hector, the war carried on, watched over by the gods, ready to take a hand in it whenever they saw fit…

A Fateful Arrow

Achilles faced Memnon, an Ethiopian king who had brought his army to the defense of Troy. Zeus weighed the souls of the two combatants and found Memnon's heavier—he had to die.

Achilles led a breakthrough into the city, but the gods judged that by now he

The death of Achilles as imagined by a 17th-century artist

had killed too many men to triumph. Paris aimed a bow towards Achilles's left heel. Apollo guided the arrow home, and Achilles fell dead. His prophecy had finally come true.

The wooden horse meant the end of the Trojans when their city was set ablaze.

The End of Troy

After ten years, the Greeks had still not won, so they built a large wooden horse, left it on the beach as a gift to the Trojans, and pretended to sail away. Hidden inside the horse were soldiers. The Trojans took the horse inside the walls. As they slept, the soldiers crept out to let in the waiting Greek army, who conquered the city.

GLOSSARY

alarmed Worried or concerned.

avenge To get revenge for a wrong committed.

bargain To make a deal.

brooded Thought negatively or worried about something for a long period of time.

charioteer A person who drives a chariot.

emboldened Filled with courage.

nymph A mythical creature resembling a woman.

pleas Urgent requests.

prophecy A prediction about the future.

pyre A raised platform on which a body is burned.

quarrel A small fight.

ramparts The topmost parts of a castle from which warriors often shot arrows or threw spears.

seer A person who has the ability to see the future.

siege An act of war in which an army surrounds the enemy's city, so the enemy cannot leave or receive supplies.

INDEX